T0402847

COUNTRY EXPLORERS

A Visit to JAPAN

by Charis Mather

BEARPORT
PUBLISHING

Minneapolis, Minnesota

Credits

All images are courtesy of Shutterstock.com, unless otherwise specified. With thanks to Getty Images, Thinkstock Photo, and iStockphoto.

Cover – julianne.hide, Guitar photographer. 2–3 – TNShutter. 4–5 – Matis75, Wathanachai Janwithayayot. 8–9 – Neale Cousland, Sean Pavone. 10–11 – Zallaz, MADSOLAR. 12–13 – Navapon Plodprong, soi7studio. 14–15 – Rido, pang_oasis. 16–17 – JenJ_Payless, oneinchpunch. 18–19 – Sean Pavone, Natapat2521. 20–21 – cowardlion, vichie81. 22–23 – Wissuta.on, Nonthachai Saksri.

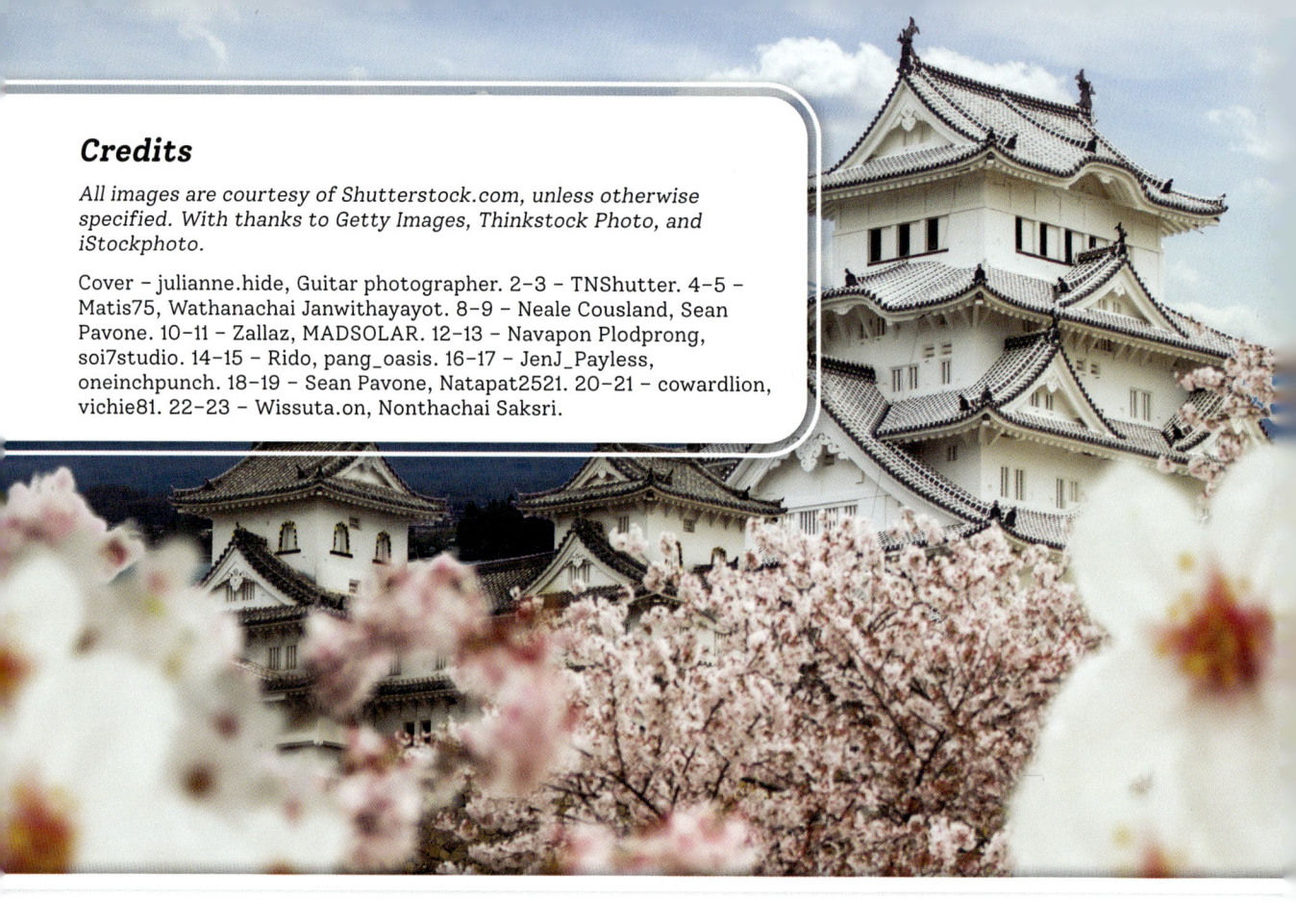

Library of Congress Cataloging-in-Publication Data is available at www.loc.gov or upon request from the publisher.

ISBN: 979-8-88509-041-4 (hardcover)
ISBN: 979-8-88509-052-0 (paperback)
ISBN: 979-8-88509-063-6 (ebook)

For more information, write to Bearport Publishing, 5357 Penn Avenue South, Minneapolis, MN 55419. Printed in the United States of America.

CONTENTS

Country to Country 4

Today's Trip Is to Japan! 6

Tokyo 8

Mount Fuji 10

Hanami 12

Food. 14

Tea Ceremony 16

Animal Parks. 18

Trains 20

Before You Go. 22

Glossary. 24

Index 24

COUNTRY TO COUNTRY

A country is an area of land marked by **borders**. The people in each country have their own rules and ways of living. They may speak different languages.

Which country do you live in?

4

Each country around the world has its own interesting things to see and do. Let's take a trip to visit a country and learn more!

Have you ever visited another country?

5

TODAY'S TRIP IS TO
JAPAN!

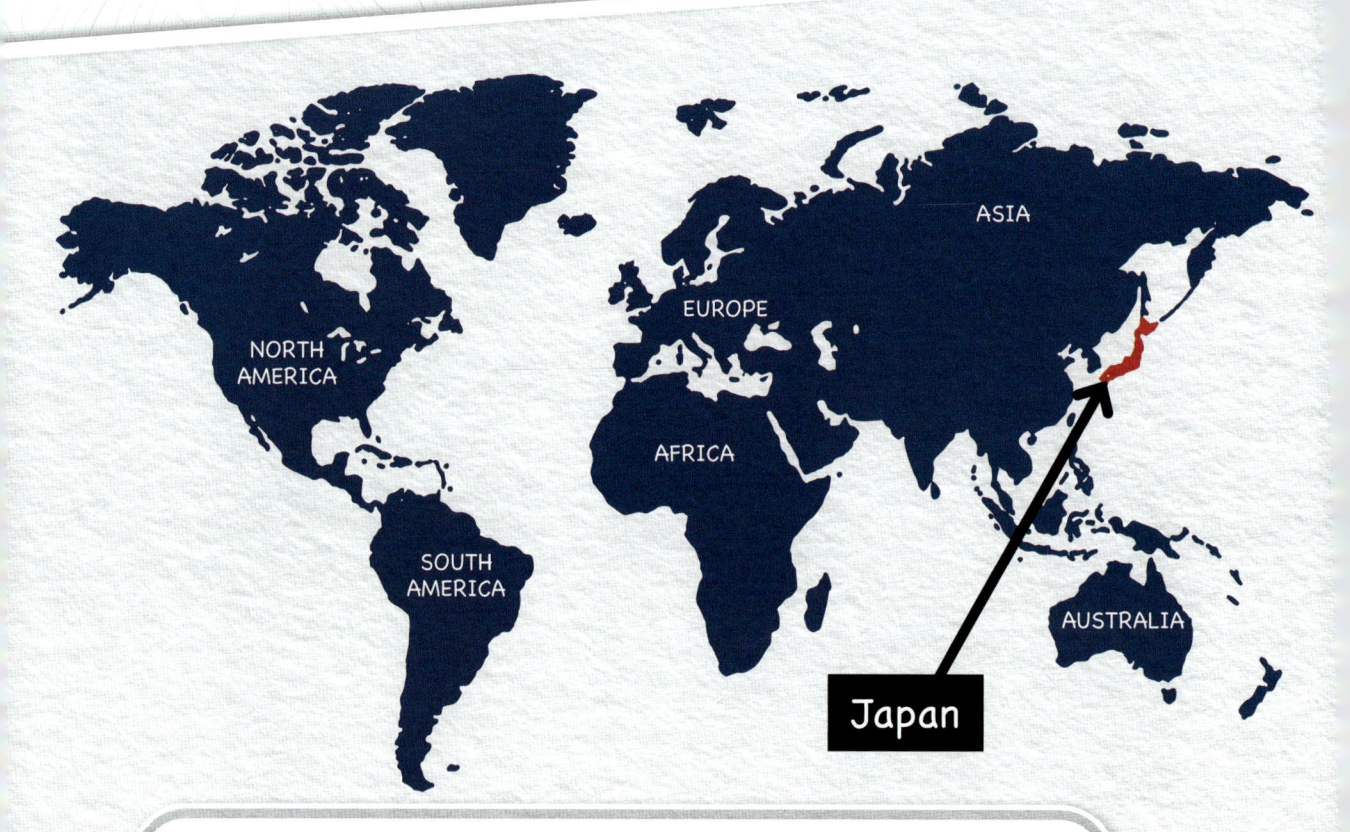

Japan

ASIA

EUROPE

NORTH AMERICA

AFRICA

SOUTH AMERICA

AUSTRALIA

Japan is a country in the **continent** of Asia.

FACT FILE

Capital city: Tokyo
Main language: Japanese
Currency: Yen
Flag:

Currency is the type of money that is used in a country.

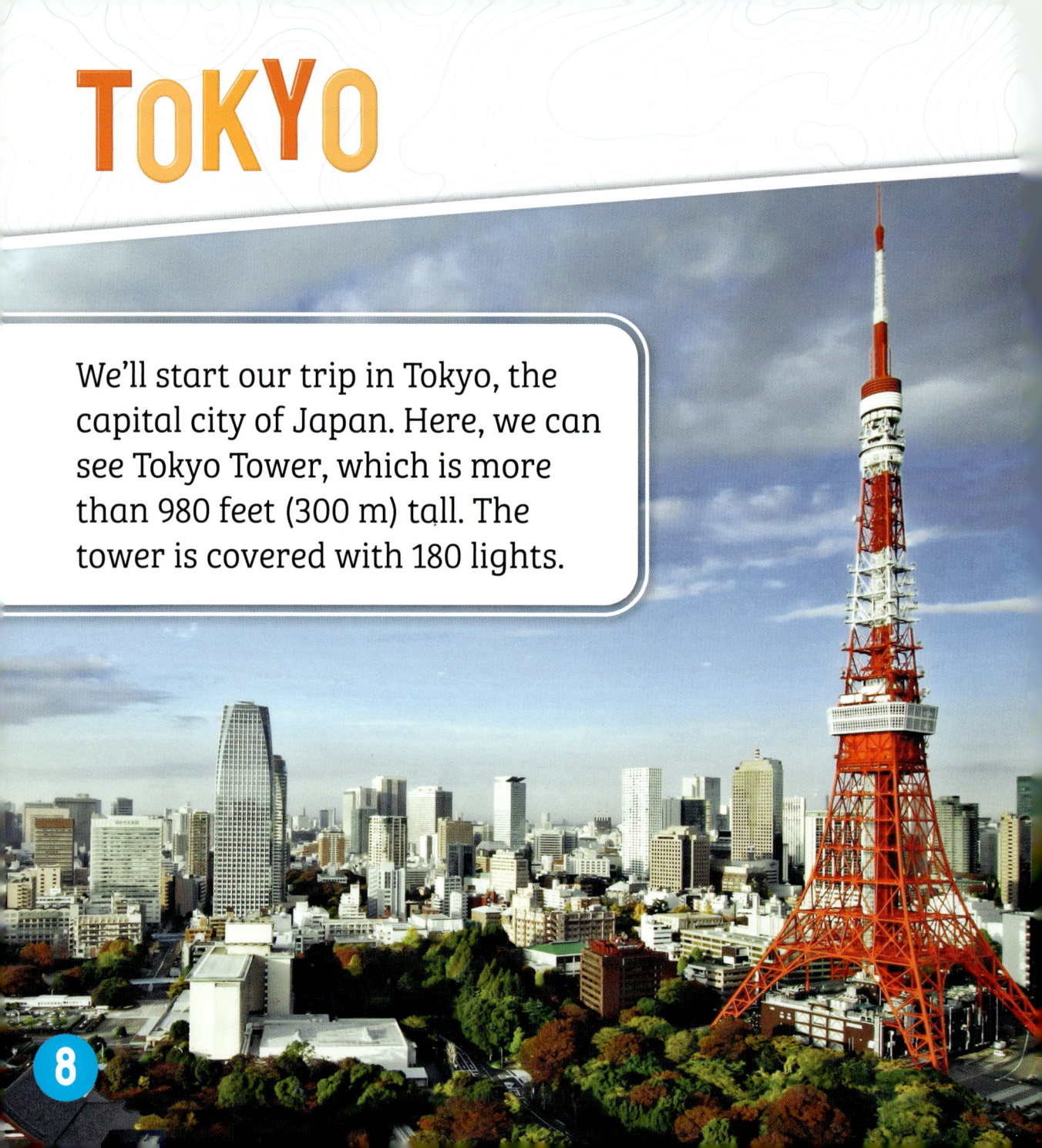

TOKYO

We'll start our trip in Tokyo, the capital city of Japan. Here, we can see Tokyo Tower, which is more than 980 feet (300 m) tall. The tower is covered with 180 lights.

8

Shibuya Crossing is one of the busiest intersections in the world.

Tokyo is a very busy city. Thousands of people get to work each day by walking through Shibuya Crossing. Every few minutes, people must stop walking to let cars drive through, too.

9

MOUNT FUJI

Many people who visit Tokyo also go to see Japan's highest mountain. Mount Fuji is more than 12,380 ft (3,770 m) tall.

Mount Fuji has snow on its top during the winter.

Mount Fuji is very important to many Japanese people, especially those who practice the **Shinto** religion. People who climb the mountain might see Shinto **shrines** on the way.

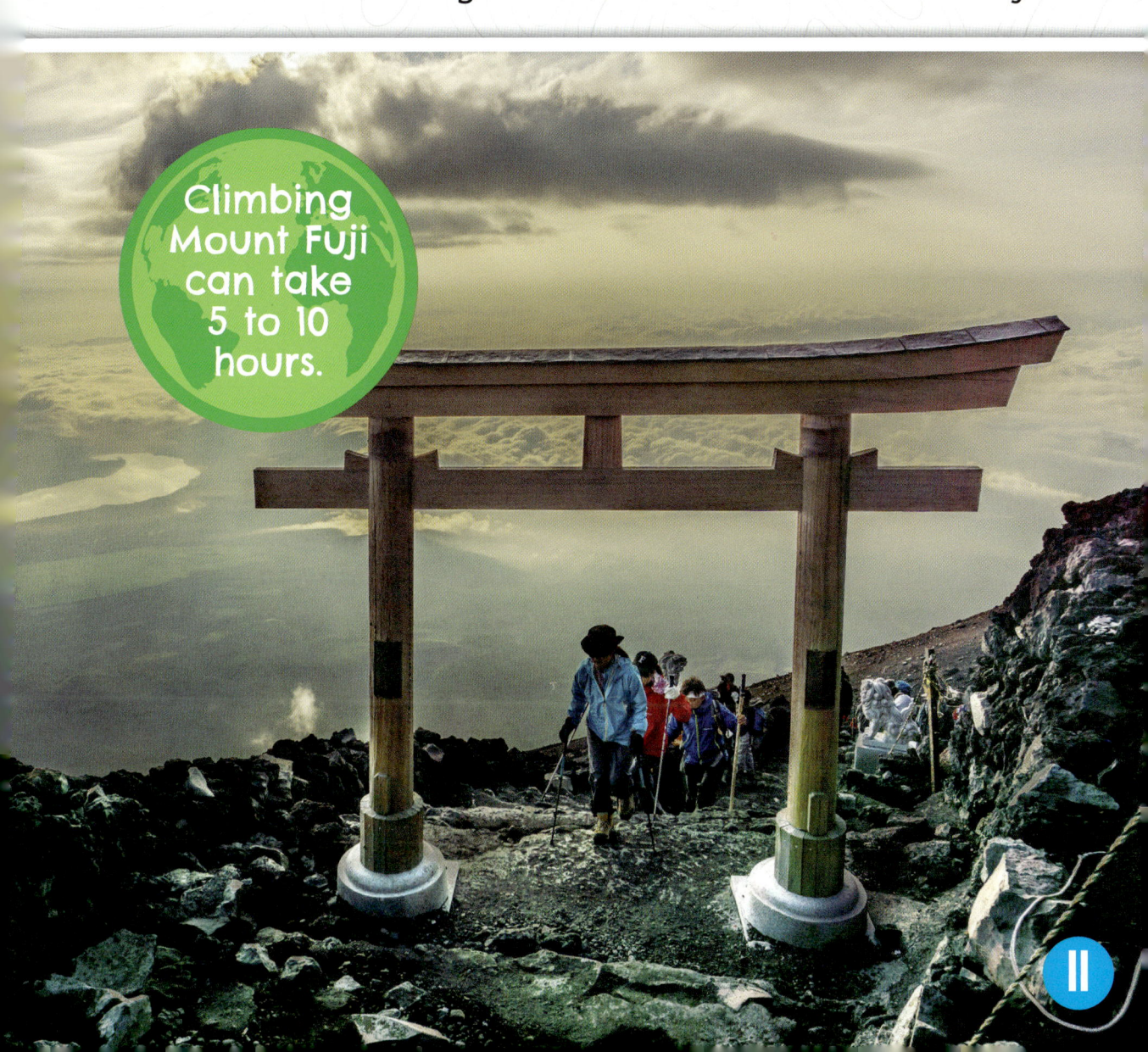

Climbing Mount Fuji can take 5 to 10 hours.

HANAMI

In the spring, many people get together to look at Japan's beautiful cherry blossom trees. Friends and families meet outside to have picnics under the blossoms. This is called *hanami*.

Hanami means flower watching in Japanese.

Cherry blossoms might last for only 10 to 14 days.

Cherry blossom trees have flowers for only a short time. During *hanami*, people watch flower petals fall from the trees. Sometimes, this looks like snow falling from the sky.

13

FOOD

Next, let's grab a bite to eat! We can try some of Japan's many fresh **seafood** dishes. Some dishes, such as sushi and sashimi, are made with **raw** fish. Japanese food often includes rice, too.

You can find many kinds of food in Japan's outdoor food stands, called *yatai*. These stands are set up to be open in the evening and moved away during the day.

Yatai serve dumplings, grilled chicken, noodles, and much more.

TEA CEREMONY

Tea is a common drink in Japan. Sometimes, it is used in special **ceremonies** to welcome guests.

A tea ceremony can last many hours.

16

There are many steps to follow in a tea ceremony. Guests sit quietly on the floor while the tea is prepared. Several tools are used to make this special tea. Once it is ready, guests drink the tea one at a time.

Tea ceremonies are very peaceful events.

ANIMAL PARKS

Jigokudani Park

In some parts of Japan, we can see animals in the wild. Jigokudani Park is sometimes called Snow Monkey Park because of the animals that live there. These monkeys often sit in pools of hot water during the winter.

Nara Park

In the city of Nara, there is a park that has hundreds of deer. These deer are used to seeing people and will often let visitors feed them.

19

TRAINS

In Japan, talking on the phone while riding a train is thought of as rude.

How should we travel around Japan? Let's take a train! We just need to be calm and quiet. Many people ride on trains in Japan. But passengers try to not bother the other people around them.

Japan's trains are some of the fastest and safest in the world. The Shinkansen train line is known for its bullet trains. These speedy trains can travel faster than 185 miles per hour (300 kph).

BEFORE YOU GO

We can't forget to see the Fushimi Inari Taisha shrine. Visitors have to walk through thousands of bright red gates to reach this Shinto shrine.

Finally, let's go to the city of Osaka, where we can see Osaka Castle. It was built a long time ago by one of Japan's **samurai** leaders.

What have you learned about Japan on this trip?

23

GLOSSARY

borders lines that show where one place ends and another begins

ceremonies meaningful events that are usually done in a similar way each time

continent one of the world's seven large land masses

raw not cooked

samurai a group of military fighters in Japan a long time ago

seafood ocean animals, such as fish or crabs, that are served as food

Shinto a Japanese religion where nature and family are important

shrines places built to honor and remember an event or being

INDEX

castles 23

deer 19

monkeys 18

mountains 10–11

shrines 11, 22

snow 10, 13, 18

Tokyo 7–10

trees 12–13